John Lewis

CHERRY LAKE PRESS

Published in the United States of America by Cherry Lake Publishing Group
Ann Arbor, Michigan
www.cherrylakepublishing.com

Reading Adviser: Marla Conn, MS Ed., Literacy specialist, Read-Ability, Inc.
Book Designer: Jennifer Wahi
Illustrator: Jeff Bane

Photo Credits: © Zurijeta/Shutterstock, 5; ©Maeven/Shutterstock, 7; ©National Archives Catalog/Photograph by Rowland Scherman/ARC ID: 542014, 9; ©National Archives Catalog/ARC ID: 542056, 11; ©Public Domain/Center for Jewish History/flickr, 13; ©Public Domain/Abernathy Family Photos/Wikimedia, 15, 22; ©Public Domain/LBJ Library photo by Yoichi Okamoto/serial no. A1031-21a, 17; ©Public Domain/National Archives/identifier 6508426, 19, 23; ©Public Domain/LBJ Library/Photo by Tony Powell/flickr, 21; Jeff Bane, Cover, 1, 8, 12, 16

Cherry Lake Press is an imprint of Cherry Lake Publishing Group.

Library of Congress Cataloging-in-Publication Data

Names: Pincus, Meeg, author. | Bane, Jeff, 1957- illustrator.
Title: John Lewis / by Meeg Pincus ; Illustrated by Jeff Bane.
Description: Ann Arbor, Michigan : Cherry Lake Publishing, [2020] | Series: My itty-bitty bio | Includes index. | Audience: Grades K-1 | Summary: "The My Itty-Bitty Bio series are biographies for the earliest readers. This book examines the life of civil rights activist John Lewis, in a simple, age-appropriate way that will help young readers develop word recognition and reading skills. Includes a table of contents, author biography, timeline, glossary, index, and other informative backmatter"-- Provided by publisher.
Identifiers: LCCN 2020037698 (print) | LCCN 2020037699 (ebook) | ISBN 9781534186361 (hardcover) | ISBN 9781534186446 (paperback) | ISBN 9781534186521 (pdf) | ISBN 9781534186606 (ebook)
Subjects: LCSH: Lewis, John, 1940-2020--Juvenile literature. | African American civil rights workers--Biography--Juvenile literature. | Civil rights workers--United States--Biography--Juvenile literature. | African Americans--Civil rights--History--20th century--Juvenile literature. | United States--Race relations--Juvenile literature.
Classification: LCC E840.8.L43 P56 2020 (print) | LCC E840.8.L43 (ebook) | DDC 323.092 [B]--dc23
LC record available at https://lccn.loc.gov/2020037698
LC ebook record available at https://lccn.loc.gov/2020037699

Printed in the United States of America
Corporate Graphics

About the author: Meeg Pincus has been a writer, editor, and educator for 25 years. She loves to write inspiring stories for kids about people, animals, and our planet. She lives near San Diego, California, where she enjoys the beach, reading, singing, and her family.

About the illustrator: Jeff Bane and his two business partners own a studio along the American River in Folsom, California, home of the 1849 Gold Rush. When Jeff's not sketching or illustrating for clients, he's either swimming or kayaking in the river to relax.

I was born in Alabama. It was 1940. I came from a big family. I had three sisters. I also had six brothers.

Black people were **segregated** during this time. I wanted to change this.

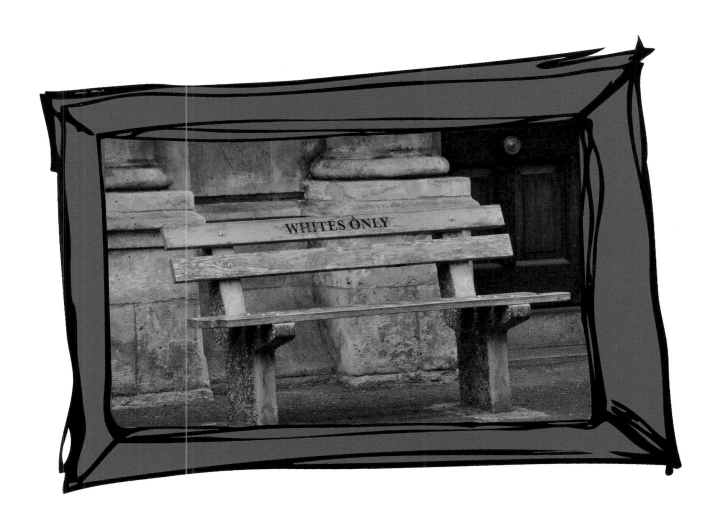

Dr. Martin Luther King Jr. led peaceful **protests** against segregation. I wrote him a letter. He invited me to help.

Who would you write a letter to?

I led many protests. People tried to use **violence** to stop me. But I answered with peace.

I planned the **March on Washington** with Dr. King.
I spoke about **equality**.
I was 23.

I led a march. There were hundreds of people. We marched for **voting rights** for Black people. We wanted to cross a bridge in Selma, Alabama. But we were attacked. I got hurt.

What would you march for?

Many Americans agreed with us. The president signed an important law. The law made it easier for Black people to vote.

I became a U.S. **congressman**.
I always worked for equality and peace.

I died in 2020. People **honored** me in Selma and in Washington, D.C. I changed the country.

What would you like to ask me?

1965

1940

Born
1940

1986

2040

Died
2020

glossary

congressman (KAHNG-gris-muhn) a man voted by his community to serve in the U.S. Congress, which makes the country's laws

equality (ih-KWAH-lih-tee) the right of everyone to be treated the same

honored (AH-nurd) praised and paid respect to

March on Washington (MAHRCH on WAH-shing-tuhn) the large 1963 civil rights protest in Washington, D.C.

protests (PROH-tests) marches or messages against something

segregated (SEG-rih-gate-id) separated from another group in an unequal way

violence (VYE-uh-luhns) the use of force to harm a person or damage property

voting rights (VOHT-ing RITES) the legal right to vote easily in an election

index